# GCD

RESOURCES TO MAKE, MATURE, AND
MULTIPLY DISCIPLES OF JESUS

## GOSPELCENTEREDDISCIPLESHIP.COM

ARTICLES | EBOOKS

People who have yet to meet Christ in a life changing way through the gospel are not stupid - they can tell if we care for them or if they are simply a project to us. In this fantastic book, Jonathan Dodson does what few books have done: he incisively slices away the failed, broken attempts to share Christ in our time without being hypercritical, opens our eyes to the beautiful and unbelievable gospel, and offers practical, biblical metaphors for sharing Christ today. We can be winsome and intentional in our witness; Jonathan shows us how. Every believer should read this!

ALVIN L. REID
Author & Professor, Southeastern Baptist Theological Seminary

Over the past decade, I've sifted through boatloads of books related to spreading the message of Christ's Gospel. I have poured slowly through the most popular books on the subject, but have always found myself longing for something more. Unbelievable Gospel contains what my heart has been yearning for, an evangelistic manifesto, that every Christian should read. It is the best evangelism book I've ever read, by far.

MATT BROWN
Author & Founder, Think Eternity

Jonathan Dodson has done something remarkable. In just under 80 pages, he confronts our evangelistic paralysis and angst with beautiful theology, real stories, and a hopeful challenge that the gospel can be compelling, contextual, and received with joy by an uninterested world. Highly recommended.

JON TYSON
Lead Pastor of Trinity Grace Church

In *Unbelievable Gospel*, Jonathan addresses many of the prevailing reasons why people don't share their faith. He does so with a balance of cultural sensibility and theological accuracy. But he does more than that, he also offers a gospel faithful way of sharing the good news to people in real need, illuminating the way forward with personal stories of success and failure in sharing a gospel worth believing. This is evangelism for the 21st century and for all centuries for that matter!

DR. ROBERT COLEMAN
Author & Professor at Gordon-Conwell Theological Seminary


We each come to the table with reasons for not sharing Jesus. Jonathan brilliantly gives us a soul-check and reminds us that evangelism can be winsome and fun when done with a heart transfixed by the person of Jesus and his work in the world. For those of us without the gift of evangelism, Jonathan encourages us that, yes, we can indeed share a believable gospel—not because of who we are or what we do, but because of what our great Savior has done for us.

LAURIE FORTUNAK NICHOLS
Managing Editor, Evangelical Missions Quarterly

# UN BEL IEV ABLE
## GOSPEL
### HOW TO SHARE A GOSPEL WORTH BELIEVING

*Jonathan K. Dodson*

AUSTIN, TEXAS

*Unbelievable Gospel*

Published by GCD Books
    1501 W 5th St, Ste 110
    Austin, TX 78703

Cover design by Josh Shank at rocketrepublic.co.

First Printing 2012
Printed in the United States of America

Trade paperback ISBN: 978-0615694924

*To George Landrum Dodson (Poppa),*
*Always an evangelist whether on his knees or in the pulpit.*

# CONTENTS

# ACKNOWLEDGEMENTS

Passion for the gospel of Jesus is only stirred up by the Spirit of Christ; however, devotion to Jesus is also catalyzed by great models - one reason why discipleship is so important. Some of the great evangelistic models in my life include: Jerry McCune, Chris Allred, Paul Dreblow, Steve Niphakis, Nate Navarro, and my grandfather, George Landrum Dodson.

I'm grateful for the editorial work and friendship of Ben Roberts, Managing Editor for Gospel Centered Discipleship.com. I'm also indebted to my church, Austin City Life, the members of which work hard to share a believable gospel. Thank you Josh Shank for your stellar design work. As always, nothing is written without the unflagging support my delightful companion and wife, Robie.

# INTRODUCTION

Evangelism has become a byword. It has fallen to the wayside in Christian vocabulary. Some see it sitting in the gutter; others walk by without noticing at all. Some have replaced it with missional; others have replaced it with social justice. Still more are aware it is there, but deliberately avoid it.

## Why Is the Gospel Good News?

Why do we avoid evangelism? The answer to this question is half the reason I wrote this book. After witnessing across the globe for thirty years, being trained with all kinds of evangelistic tools, and making disciples in the local church, I have discovered a fundamental question is often overlooked—"How is the gospel good news to those we evangelize?" Evangelicals are proficient at rehearsing the information of the gospel but we often lack the ability to situate the gospel in the lives of others. We need to get into their skin, to understand how the gospel could transform the self-righteous do-gooder, the skeptical urbanite, the abused mother, the successful professional, and the strung out addict. It is true that, in the end, the Holy Spirit has the final say in convincing others that the gospel is good news. But it is also true that the Holy Spirit chooses to use what we say along the way.

The gospel is good news whether someone perceives it to be good to them or not. But the only reason *we* know is because we experience its grace-saturated goodness in *our* everyday lives. We know the gospel is good, not just in theory, but in the experience of suffering, parenting, dating, working, and so on. For instance, we know the gospel is good because it frees us from being a slave to other's opinions, when through faith in Christ, we have obtained the opinion that matters most—God the Father saying, "This is my son. I am pleased with you!" This deep, undying love and approval of God the Father frees us from people-pleasing, over-working, spouse-impressing, self-adoring living. The gospel sets us free! The trouble, of course, is that there are so many people who don't know the power of the gospel like you and me. They don't know *how* the gospel is good news for *them*.

If Jesus did die and rise for the world, then it is incumbent upon his followers to tell them how and why the gospel is good. Reciting the memorized fact that Jesus died on the cross for sins to a coworker doesn't tell them why this important or how it can change their life. Reciting this information dispassionately is even less convincing. What people need to know is not only what the gospel is but also what the gospel does. Asking people to believe in the death and resurrection of a first century Jewish messiah, for no apparent reason, is quite unbelievable. The problem we face, then, is not simply an issue of bad press, but also an issue of how to share the gospel in a way that is worth believing. But in order to do that, *we* have to find the gospel something worth believing.

## Recovering from Evangelism

Evangelism is something many twenty-first century Christians are trying to recover from. It often stirs up memories of rehearsed presentations, awkward door-to-door witnessing, or even forced conversions in revival-like settings. To be certain, God has used these efforts but not as much as is often claimed.[1] Regardless, those results were based on a modernist worldview in a culture familiar with Christianity. The evangelism of the twentieth century was based on common assumptions like: the brute fact of absolute truth, the existence of heaven and hell (or

---

[1] One such example, comes from the Harvest Crusades of evangelist Greg Laurie: "Greg Laurie's staff estimates that 16,000 conversions occurred at Harvest Christian Fellowship in the five-year period from 1986 to 1991. . . . Perhaps only 10 percent of these decisions resulted in long-term changes in personal behavior." Donald Miller, *Reinventing American Protestantism: Christianity in the New Millennium* (Berkeley: Univ. of California Press, 1997), 171-72 cited in Richard Peace, "Conflicting Understandings of Christian Conversion: A Missiological Challenge" IBMR, Vol. 28, No.1. *Jan* 2004, 8.

God for that matter), and a widely held notion that sin keeps us from God. Those assumptions can no longer be assumed. Today, many Christian teachings and assumptions are fuzzy, even questionable, for society at large. Calling people to "repent and believe in Jesus" could be easily construed as "stop doing bad things, start doing good things (like Jesus did), and God will save you." This, of course, is nowhere close to the aim of biblical evangelism. Biblical evangelism focuses on communicating our need to respond to Jesus Christ as Lord of all, not on how we can get God to respond to our moral performance. The gospel is bigger and smaller than most people think, as big as the cosmos and as small as you and me. It is the good and true news that Jesus has defeated sin, death, and evil through his own death and resurrection and is making all things new, even us! The challenge before the church is to put that epic definition of the gospel into the "even us" in a way that is personal, meaningful, coherent, and believable. To show people *how* Jesus is better.

## Getting to a Believable Gospel

In order to recover a believable evangelism, we must do two things. First, we must consider *why evangelism is so often avoided*. This question occupies half of the book. Along the way, I consider five types of unbelievable evangelism that lead many to avoid sharing their faith. Evangelism that is: preachy, impersonal, intolerant, know-it-all, and shallow. Second, we must understand *how the gospel is worth believing for those around us*. This question fills the other half of the book. Taking up five major gospel metaphors (justification, union with Christ, redemption, adoption, new creation), I try to show how these different gospel images or doctrines can be applied to different people in different circumstances. In order for our evangelism to be believable, it must be biblical. When communicating the gospel of grace, we must draw on biblical truths, stories, and images. Stop there, however, and we fail to communicate how the gospel is good news *to others*. Like good counselors, we must listen to others well in order to know how to effectively communicate the unsearchable riches of Christ in a way that makes sense. By addressing genuine evangelistic concerns, and charting a practical way forward, I hope the Lord will use this book to stoke fresh fires of belief in the gospel for both Christians and not yet Christians. Perhaps this modest investment will assist in moving evangelism from a byword to a believable word.

# 1

## Is Your Gospel Unbelievable?

Many people find the gospel of Jesus Christ simply unbelievable. Contrary to what you might think, there are many good reasons for their unbelief.

I first met Ben at state rehab center. As I approached an 80's style, one-story house, I quickly realized the gravity of the moment. Met by an officer, I was instructed to leave all my belongings in the car, especially my cell phone. After making it through registration and a painful advocate video, I was released to talk to Ben. We went outside to a stretch of land where grass barely grew. It was sprinkled with trees providing some shade from the Texas heat. Ben made his way over to a cracked, stone table and sat down on the bench. The cemetery-like outdoor furniture was foreboding. Smoke hung in the air. I joined Ben, sitting on a bench directly across from him. Bloated and nervous he looked at me. I opened our conversation by saying: "Hi, Ben, thank you for allowing me to visit you today." After some small talk, I inquired: "Ben, I know this isn't the script you wrote for your life. It's not what you dreamed of as a kid. Tell me how you got here. I want to hear your story." Reaching back to his childhood, Ben shared experiences of rejection. He spoke of being different, not accepted, and feeling a deep loneliness. Drugs offered him escape from loneliness and entrance into a new, accepting community of users. Along the way, he discovered that community was more about sharing "highs" than sharing life. There were limits to their acceptance. Aware of the shortcomings of his drug community, Ben tried to numb the pain with more aggressive drugs.

Before he knew it, ten years had flown by. Here he was, in rehab and on probation, sitting across from a pastor he had only met once. Ben had been raised in church and knew about Jesus, but he had never found the gospel truly believable. Growing up, he had been told Jesus died on the cross for him, but church had been a place of rejection not acceptance. Based on his experience with God's people, the gospel wasn't really something worth believing. In fact, he had moved onto atheism. As I listened to him, I thought to myself: "How do I talk about Jesus in a way that meets Ben where he is? What do I tell a broken, lonely, anxious, recovering addict? 'Don't worry, Ben, just believe Jesus died on the cross and everything will be okay.'?" Ben clearly needed more than a memorized fact about Jesus. How could I communicate the hope of Christ in a meaningful, personal way? How could we get beyond the un-believability of the gospel he encountered when he was young to a gospel that really is worth believing?

Most of us share an unbelievable gospel. We cough up memorized information about Jesus that has little apparent meaning for life. If we're honest, we don't exactly know *how* Jesus is good news for others; we just *believe* he is. This poses a problem for people who don't share our mindless belief. "Just believe in Jesus," we say, but what we tell them is so unbelievable! They can't conceive how the death of a first century, Jewish messiah could be good news to them. Alternatively, their best news seems to trump our good news. How can we share the gospel in way that is compelling? This is where our calling to "do the work of an evangelist" comes in (2 Tim. 4:5).

There are so many unbelievable evangelists. In popular culture, evangelists are mocked for their hypocrisy, plasticity, and idolatry. Their sermons on the good news are unbelievable because their functional belief is in different news. Instead of the satisfaction of the Savior, they are sold out to the satisfaction of sex, comfort, and wealth. Instead of resting in the acceptance of Jesus, they restlessly seek the acceptance of the masses through power-hungry crusades for influence and fame. These evangelists are utterly unbelievable. But they aren't the only incredible evangelists.

The workplace crusaders and angry street preachers who campaign to convert co-workers to their doctrine or recruit bystanders to their politics are also unbelievable. Even the well-intentioned evangelical who looks to get Jesus off his chest and into conversation is unbelievable. Too many Christians look to clear their evangelistic conscience by simply mentioning the name of Jesus or saying that he died on the cross for sins. Saying Jesus' name in conversation earns us a √. Mentioning what Jesus did (on the cross) earns us a √+. This performance-based approach to evangelism is incredible because it fails to embody the truth we preach. Dismissing people's struggles, fears, hopes, and reasons for unbelief, we plow onward with our name-dropping. This is unbelievable. People can sense when they are approached as an evangelistic box to check on our spiritual checklist. No one likes to be a project. Unbelievable evangelists actually create more obstacles than opportunities for the gospel.

This is a book on evangelism, though I struggle to use that word because of all its baggage. More importantly, it is about the gospel of Jesus Christ. The gospel is both bigger and smaller than we think. Sometimes we can't imagine the scope of the gospel, as news so good that it changes everything—society, culture, and creation. People really need to hear this. This vision of reality is better than anyone can imagine. The good news of the gospel is better than the best news people can conceive.

Others times, we can't imagine the subtlety of the gospel, that it brings us exactly what we need in Christ: acceptance, approval, forgiveness, newness, healing, worth, purpose, joy, hope, peace, and freedom, all in Jesus. The gospel is bigger and smaller than we think, as big as the cosmos and as small as you and me. It is the good and true news that Jesus has defeated sin, death, and evil through his own death and resurrection and is making all things new, even us! I have limited the scope of this book to the smaller expression of the gospel, though the grandiosity of the gospel is also important and effective in evangelism. This short book combines evangelism with cultural apologetics. It is mainly practical, focusing on how we can better communicate the gospel better to others. True to the original meaning of evangelism, this book is about how we herald the good news of Jesus Christ.

All disciples are called to evangelism, but an evangelist isn't someone who coughs up information about Jesus or proselytizes people. According to Paul, an evangelist is someone who communicates the gospel of Jesus with patience and wisdom. This is why it is "work"—not because it is onerous but because it requires thoughtfulness. Anyone can drop a name or recite a presentation, but it takes effort to listen patiently to discern how to share the gospel in a wise and meaningful way. The great cultural apologist-evangelist, Francis Schaeffer, was asked what he would say if he had an hour to share the gospel with someone. He responded by saying: "I will spend the first fifty-five minutes asking questions and finding out what is troubling their heart and mind, and then in the last five minutes will I share something of the truth."[2] The work or calling of an evangelist isn't to drop names, recite presentations, or campaign politics. Rather, the work of the evangelist is to listen patiently for minutes, hours, days, weeks, and years in order to wisely show others how the gospel is actually *worth* believing.

## Is Unbelief the Only Problem?

Christians persuaded of Reformed theology will be quick to point out that the real reason people don't believe the gospel is because they are depraved "unbelievers." Before we jump to the cold-hearted conclusion that the reason people don't believe is because they are depraved, we do well to listen to the wisdom of Paul and follow the example of Jesus. Both Paul and Jesus shared the good news wisely and patiently with others. Paul "reasoned boldly" with Jews and Greeks (Acts 17:2, 17; 18:4, 19). He told the Christians to: "Walk in wisdom toward outsiders, making the best use of the time. Let your speech always be gracious, seasoned with salt, so that you may know how you ought to answer each person" (Col. 4:5). Knowing that people are depraved didn't prevent Paul from treating them with

---

[2] Jerram Barrs, "Francis Schaeffer: The Man and His Message" November 2006. *Reformation 21*, 14-15. See also his helpful books: *The Heart of Evangelism* and *Learning Evangelism from Jesus.*

respect and dignity. In fact, it was his awareness that every human bears God's image that led him to reason in wisdom, patience, and love.

Jesus also listened and reasoned. He selected gospel metaphors that were appropriate to his hearers, using agricultural imagery with villagers (Luke 13), legal imagery with lawyers (Luke 11:37-54), spiritual birth with law-keeping Pharisees (John 3:1-8), and even water for people who were thirsty (John 4:1-34), but both Paul and Jesus were well aware of the condition of their listeners' hearts. Paul describes our hearts as darkened (Rom. 1:21), boxed up in a coffin (Eph 2:1), dead and lifeless. Without the shining light of the gospel of glory of Christ (2 Cor. 4:4), darkened hearts aren't illuminated and dead bodies don't truly live. The problem, however, is that through our mindless, impatient, and unwise evangelism, we pile stones on top of their graves. Good evangelism removes the stones and shares the truth in such a way that the good news can travel down the shaft of gospel light into darkened hearts. When we share an unbelievable gospel, we refuse to address reasons for unbelief. We refuse to remove the stones. We stop up our ears and demand blind faith, but unbelief has its reasons. Like Ben, people have reasons for not believing the gospel of Jesus. Reasons range from intellectual doubt to perceiving no existential value in Christianity. This is where Jesus-like evangelists come in. Joining the Spirit, we can roll up our sleeves, listen for hours, and remove the stones. While God alone opens the heart, we must be ready to breathe a believable gospel into their lives. Only then will we recover a way of communicating the gospel that embodies the gospel—patiently, wisely, and lovingly—revealing the beauty and believability of Jesus.

This book explores two primary things. First, we will consider *why* our gospel is unbelievable. It is unbelievable, not only because of the content of our evangelism but also how we evangelize. To be frank, the gospel is not believable because of the way we share it. There are many Christians who have actually stopped sharing their faith because the way they have been taught to share the gospel is shot through with un-believability. These Christians have shared life with enough "unbelievers" to know that, while unbelief in the gospel is finally a matter of the heart, it is intermediately a matter of communication. All too often, Christians communicate a canned, insincere or judgmental message. Believers have seen too many stones piled on the hearts of genuine, thoughtful, struggling unbelievers. These Christians see reasons why *not* to share their faith. Second, we will consider *how* to share a gospel worth believing. It is not enough to simply see why we shouldn't share our faith or to expose evangelistic errors. We need to learn all we can through critique but move forward to construct a form of evangelism that is truly believable. To this end, I commend

Gospel Metaphors, a way of sharing the gospel connected to real life that is based on the various gospel images in Scripture. Before we move into this two-prong focus, it is important to address *the topic of evangelism.*

## Why You Shouldn't Share the Gospel

I mentioned that there are good reasons why people don't believe the gospel. Many of these reasons have to do with errors in evangelistic efforts. The errors include: proselytizing, preachy self-righteousness, antagonism toward other faiths, shallow presentations, and proud know-it-all attitudes. These approaches to sharing the gospel are quite the opposite of the gospel of grace because they smack with disrespect, hubris, and insincerity. Each of these errors is mirrored by an evangelistic concern. The concerns are precisely why many evangelicals have stopped sharing their faith. Evangelistic concerns include: not being preachy, not being impersonal, not being intolerant, and not being a know-it-all. These concerns can be loving, humble, and thoughtful reasons why people *don't* share their faith. If the first group of errors characterizes your evangelistic activity, then you may need to stop sharing your faith. If you share the second set of concerns, then you probably need to *start* sharing your faith (if you're not already). The person with self-righteous conviction needs to stop sharing their faith, while the person with loving concerns needs to start sharing their faith. The former group is unbelievable, while the latter could be believable. The wrong people are sharing their faith!

I'm not trying to be provocative. Well, perhaps a bit. To clarify, when I say you have reason to *not* share your faith, I am questioning the faith that is being shared. When the self-righteous preachy person talks down to others about Jesus, they express functional faith in something other than Jesus. Preaching with an attitude of superiority, they preach any number of isms: Moralism: "If you are moral like me, then God will accept you." Spiritualism: "If you practiced spirituality like me, then you would find Jesus." Politicism: "If you held my political views, then God would be on your side." When a disciple has faith in a false gospel, their lives speak louder than their words. Their false gospel bleeds through their evangelizing. As a result, they share a functional faith in a false lord not actual faith in the one, true Lord. To be clear, I am not suggesting that people shouldn't share their faith at all. What I am suggesting is that when we are motivated by something other than faith in Jesus, we may not be sharing the gospel. Take, for instance, the person who attempts to proselytize a co-worker. The Christian may put faith in their argumentation or right doctrine, not in Jesus. They think to themselves: "If I can shoot down all their objections and then get them to church, then they will become a Christian." Notice this line of thinking has nothing to do with Jesus. Rather, it has everything to do with getting people to embrace your doctrine and join your church. This is called proselytizing not evangelism.

## Evangelism is Not Proselytizing

Proselytizing is motivated by recruitment. Those who proselytize try to recruit people to different things. Take beliefs or church for instance. The proselytizer puts faith in rational arguments and in social networks. He thinks to himself, "If I can just disprove my coworkers belief system and expose them to a lot of people who have my beliefs, then they will be swept into Christianity." Whatever is of greatest value to us will motivate our proselytizing. Depending on your values, Christianity may have its strongest expression in a political party, a moral code, a view of the book of Revelation, a form or denomination of church, or a doctrinal stance. Notice that none of these values are focused on Jesus. We all recruit to what we think is most important. Men recruit to sports teams; women recruit to fashion trends. In the case of the proselytizer, he recruits to faith in a messiah and lord other than Jesus. On the whole, faith is placed in the messiah of church and the lord of doctrine. This false gospel goes something like: "If you join the right church and get the right doctrine, then you can be saved." The true gospel simply says: "If you join Jesus through repentance and faith, he will save you." Quite different.

The proselytizer's good news is that you can swap out your inferior beliefs and community for her superior beliefs and better community (which is offensive). This approach demeans people who have strong friendships and sincere beliefs, but more disturbingly, it points them to faith in a false god. It teaches people to trust in believing the right things and joining the right church. Church and doctrine make for very bad gods and will eventually disappoint. Trust me, I see disillusioned people come and go from churches because their real faith is in the people or a pet doctrine, not in Jesus. The Church isn't meant to bear the weight of our spiritual hunger for security and relational connectedness; God is—Father, Son and Spirit. This misplaced faith is why I'm suggesting Christian proselytizers *not* share their faith. They are not sharing "the faith that was once for all delivered to the saints" (Jude 3). Simply put, the recruiter should not share their faith because their faith is not the gospel of Jesus.

Does this mean we have to get our hearts just right before we share the gospel? After all, Paul rejoiced even when Christ was preached from selfish ambition, from deceptive motives (Phil. 1:17-18). We all fluctuate in our motivation for evangelism. But proselytizing Christians don't simply share from wrong motives; they share the wrong gospel: "Believe what I believe and hang out with whomever I hang out with, and God will save you." "Get your church or doctrine right and God will save you." Anathema. Again, I am not trying to keep people from sharing the gospel. What I'm suggesting is that we need to consider what kind of gospel we are sharing. Even deeper, why are we sharing it? I am advocating that we share the true gospel, namely that Jesus is the Christ and the one, true Lord, the only Messiah that redeems from sin and the true King that reigns over all. The gospel is news about the good and true story that Jesus has defeated sin, death, and evil through his own death and resurrection and is making all things new, even us. Faith in that gospel sweeps us, not into Christianity but into Christ. It offers us an entirely new way of being human, not merely a new way of thinking and behaving (any religion can do that).

When the gospel is preached, it calls for repentance and faith in Jesus (Mk. 1:14-15; Rom. 9:9). Repentance is nothing short of an identity shift based on a shift in faith. Biblical faith is not in a new set of beliefs and friends; it is much deeper than that. It is a shift that comes about through an exchange of one identity for another, from an old identity to a new identity "in Christ." The gospel says: "God saves you, not by faith in your doctrine and friends, but based on faith in Jesus." Faith in other things will bring a slow, disappointing death, but faith in Jesus pulls us into a deeply satisfying life. Since the gospel is an exchange of death for life, not an exchange of wrong beliefs for right beliefs, it must change where we place our faith. The gospel is not about recruitment to a cause or community; it is about regeneration to a new Savior and Lord. Therefore, when we share the faith, we get to share faith in something that actually changes our whole person not just our beliefs or friends. The gospel requires much more than mere belief, a switch in doctrines; it requires faith, a switch in saviors.

## Why this is Important for Everyone

After spending almost fifteen years in creative class cities where Christianity is typically marginalized and misunderstood, I've noticed that each city possesses its own unique challenges to communicating the gospel. Some of these challenges have led Christians to quiet down and let their actions do the preaching. Yet, there remains an intellectual and spiritual responsibility to communicate what we believe to those who would hear us. Whether it's diversity-proud Minneapolis, intellectually elite Boston, or creatively weird Austin, I've noticed some reasons for not sharing my faith have travelled with me from city to city. I have also observed that many other Christians share these evangelistic concerns. Left unaddressed, these concerns leave us in a state of limbo. We wonder: "Is my concern legitimate or not?" "How should I share the gospel given my concerns?" Some of these concerns deserve lengthier treatment that this booklet can afford.

I will focus our attention on five evangelistic concerns, which often make the gospel unbelievable: 1) preachy evangelism, 2) impersonal evangelism, 3) intolerant evangelism, 4) know-it-all evangelism, and 5) shallow evangelism. In addition, I will describe a way to share the gospel in a more believable way. Responding to each concern, I will use five gospel metaphors to describe how we can communicate a believable gospel: 1) justification, 2) union with Christ, 3) redemption, 4) adoption, and 5) new creation. Each chapter will also include a story of how I have used gospel metaphors to share a gospel worth believing. I have not arrived in evangelism. I am not the consummate apologist. I do the work of an evangelist and put the results in God's hands. As I do, I am learning more every day. I hope this booklet will contribute to a more patient, wise, and believable evangelism. I also hope that it will prove useful in training disciples in a simple, biblical way, to communicate the most important message in human history—the gospel of Jesus Christ.

## 2

## I Don't Want to Be Preachy

One of the reasons people often find it difficult to share their faith is because they don't want to be perceived as preachy. This is a good concern. Preachy Christians often turn people away from Christ. Think of snarky, self-righteous Angela from *The Office*. Quick to judge everyone in the office, she jumps on every opportunity to be right and show everyone else they are wrong. In one episode, she snaps at Pam's remark about needing more "loaves and fishes," referring to needing more food for a party. Angela retorts: "Jesus is not your caterer." Thanks for the clarification, Angela. She's spiritually superior and beneath her self-righteous attitude lurks a deep hypocrisy. Angela sleeps with Dwight and then cheats on him with Andy, all as a self-proclaimed Christian. Angela is the last thing a disciple of Jesus wants to be associated with—preachy and hypocritical. Many Christians hesitate to bring up spiritual matters because they don't want to be perceived as self-righteous. This concern isn't limited to fictional characters. Street preachers can also create a preachy impression of Christianity. Remember the free speech fundamentalist yellers on campus in college? I remember watching them. They stood on a box to yell. They looked down on the rest of us, sounding off with hell, fire, and damnation.

These preachy, Christian types all share something in common— self-righteousness. If we're honest, we all have a bit of self-righteousness in us, but with these types it's amplified. We hesitate to talk about Jesus because we don't want to be associated with them. We're concerned it would turn others off. But our concern should run even deeper. Preachy self-righteousness isn't just a turn off; it's the opposite of the gospel. This brings into focus our first, principal concern: We should avoid preachy self-righteousness because it communicates something opposite to the gospel.

Preachy self-righteousness says: "If you perform well (morally or spiritually), God will accept you." But the gospel says, "God already accepts you because Jesus performed perfectly on your behalf." There's a hell of difference between the two. The gospel sets us free from performance and releases us into the arms of grace. Self-wrought performance is a death sentence, but the obedience of Christ on our behalf is eternal life. What people need to hear is grace, audacious, seems-too-good-to-be-true but so-true-its-good, grace. Grace is God working his way down to us, so that we don't have to work our way up to him. He comes down to us in Jesus. We need to make Jesus the stumbling block, not preachy self-righteousness or spiritual performance.

## Changing the "Preachy" Perception

Now, there's also a critical response to this concern. While it's true that we should oppose preachy self-righteousness (because it obscures the gospel of grace), it is also true that the gospel offends our own self-righteous sensibilities. The gospel reminds us that we don't have what it takes before a holy God, that Christ alone has what it takes, and that he died and rose to give it to us. The gospel is offensive; it lifts up a mirror to show us who we really are, but it is also redemptive; it lifts up Christ to show us who we can become. In the shining light of God's glory, our darkness becomes quickly apparent. We can feel it. Deep down, something is wrong, bent, even broken. We're in need of repair. We spend most of our lives trying to avoid this inner sense, which distorts us even more.

The gospel helps us see ourselves as we are, but offers us an entirely new image, the image of the glory of God shining in the face of Jesus Christ. If we give up on ourselves and give into Jesus, he'll exchange our darkness for his light, our distortion for his beauty. This is news worth sharing. The problem, however, isn't just that people think "preachy self-righteousness" when they hear the word "gospel." It's that this concern can mute the gospel. In thoughtful consideration, we quiet down to let our actions do the preaching but, in the end, people hear nothing. When Christians press mute, people are left to make up their own versions of Christianity. We think our silence will remedy the perception of self-righteousness, but silence, instead of sharing, doesn't offer a remedy.

One day I was having a congenial chat with a man in Starbucks, until he asked what I was doing. I responded, "I'm working on a sermon." He replied by waving his hands, one across another, saying "Oh, no. I don't want to hear the sermon. Don't preach to me!" This was followed by a nervous chuckle. I should have "preached" the gospel to him but I didn't want to come off "preachy." The true aim of preaching isn't meant to mound up all our woes and make us feel guilty. Preaching is meant to relieve your woes and remove your guilt through faith in Jesus. Similarly, the gospel doesn't just show us who we really are; it shows us who we can become in Christ. Sure, it lifts up a mirror but it also lifts up Christ, raising us up with him in hope. Our concern to avoid preachy self-righteousness is good, but we have not gone far enough to remove this religious visage. How will the incorrect view of Christianity be corrected? Actions might remedy a perception of personal self-righteousness, but they can't correct a religious view of the gospel. Only words can clarify the meaning of the gospel. Paul reminds us: "And how are they to believe in him of whom they have never heard? And how are they to hear without someone preaching?" (Rom. 10:14). People won't be able to get past preachy images of religion unless someone "preaches" a message of grace to them. No one just comes up with grace. In fact, most religions come up with works, a way to work your way into Nirvana, the Brahman, or Heaven. Only in the gospel of Christ does God work his way down to us. How, then, can we enter into gospel conversations in ways that are biblically faithful and personally meaningful to those around us? What we need is *gospel metaphors.*

## Gospel Metaphors

The Scriptures contain numerous gospel metaphors. These metaphors stretch across the breadth of the Bible, Old Testament to New Testament, communicating God's saving grace. They collect in the epistles as: justification, redemption, adoption, new creation, and union with Christ.[3] These gospel metaphors bring a train of transformative graces to us in Jesus. They pull into the station by virtue of our union with Christ. All of these blessings are mediated to us through our union with Christ, the station through which the train of graces passes. Union with Christ is the essential, integrating gospel metaphor.

---

[3] Redemption contains a subset of gospel metaphors including: atonement, reconciliation, and propitiation.

Through faith in Jesus, God offers us a new identity informed by the graces present in each gospel metaphor. These graces are not metaphors in the sense that they are symbolic of some deeper reality. Rather, each gospel metaphor actually represents a facet of the gospel. For example, justification presents how a holy God can relate to sinful men and women and still remain holy. It is how a righteous God relates to unrighteous people by making them righteous. Justification does not explain how we become part of God's family (adoption), receive forgiveness (redemption), escape his wrath (reconciliation/propitiation), or how we gain a new identity (new creation/regeneration). Each gospel metaphor conveys a unique blessing from the Father. All of the metaphors converge in the good news concerning Jesus and reveal how the Father, Son, and Spirit collaborate for our restored, renewed humanity. Impressively, these metaphors are also applied to the renewal of all creation, though that is not our focus here.[4] The gospel is massively relevant to everyone and everything.

---

[4] Each gospel metaphor has a bigger application to the cosmos indicating that belief in the gospel obtains a future we all want, a renewed heavens and earth. Reflecting on *new creation*, Jesus speaks of the regeneration of the world (Matt. 19:28). In terms of *justification*, Peter describes a new heavens and earth where everything is "put to rights" or where righteous dwells (2 Pet. 3:13). The *adoption* of the sons of God is a trigger for the healing of all creation (Rom. 8:18-25). Finally, the whole world is reconciled to God by the blood of Jesus' cross (Col. 1:20). Although beyond the scope of this book, the cosmic dimension of the gospel is of tremendous value in evangelism.

For our purposes, I will show how each gospel metaphor can be used to talk about Jesus in ways that are culturally appropriate and personally meaningful. If we do the work of understanding gospel metaphors, and listen carefully to people's stories, we can discern how to best communicate the gospel in a believable way. Each chapter will raise a concern in evangelism. After considering the merits and demerits of each concern, I will share a story of how I applied a specific gospel metaphor in a real situation. Regarding the concern of preachy self-righteousness, we turn to the gospel metaphor of justification.

## Sharing a Different Righteousness

People pick up on preachy, self-righteous Christianity. I have a non-Christian friend who had very little exposure to church. When he found out I am a "preacher"; he had a lot of questions. Most of all, he and his family were just happy to have found some new friends. As we got to know each other through parties, lunches, and coffees, he eventually began bringing his family to Sunday gatherings. We continued to talk. Eventually, he started reading books about the gospel and even visited one of our City Groups. He had a lot of exposure to the gospel through our Christian community. Naturally, I was curious where he was with Jesus. One day over lunch I asked him: "So, John, how are things with Jesus?" John launched into some challenges he was facing. "I'll never be like my moral superior at work," he said.

He described the challenge of Christianity, as he saw it: "I'm just trying to climb that spiritual ladder, man; I'm just not doing that well." As I listened, I empathized with his struggle and looked directly at him. I wanted him to know that, despite his struggles and wrong answers, he had a real friend.

After he was finished, I expressed more empathy and offered to help him with some employment challenges. Then I said: "John, would it be alright if I picked up on a couple things you said about your spiritual struggle? I noticed that when I asked you about how things were going with Jesus, you described your moral superior at work and the difficulty of climbing the spiritual ladder. I really admire your effort, but I've got some bad news: You'll never be moral enough for a perfect, holy God. I could never be moral enough, either, but the good news is that Jesus climbed down the spiritual ladder to die for all your moral failures, offer you forgiveness, raise from the dead, and if you'll trust him, he will put you on his back, climb all the way up the spiritual ladder, and place you in front of a holy God, fully loved and fully accepted. That, John, is what Jesus has to do with your life." With wonder on his face, John looked right at me and said: "Is it really that easy?" I had to pause a minute. "Yes, it really is that easy." Give up on yourself and give into Jesus and you'll find perfect acceptance.

Using John's language, and responding to *his* struggle, I got past preachy self-righteousness by communicating a different righteousness. Noticing he struggled with the very thing that many Christians reinforce—religious performance for God's acceptance—I saw how Christ's performance for God's acceptance was precisely what he needed to hear. Now, I could have picked any gospel metaphor, redemption or new creation, but listening well, I discerned the metaphor that would mean the most to him. By applying the gospel of justification to his very real struggle of moral performance, I was able to make an unbelievable gospel believable. It was believable for him because he saw how the good news was helpful for him in his bad news. By listening well to others' struggles, we can make an unbelievable gospel, good, believable, news.

# 3

# I Don't Want to Be Impersonal

Another reason we often find it difficult to share the gospel is because we want to form relationships first. We don't want to be impersonal. Avoiding preachy self-righteousness, we try to get to know others before talking about Jesus. We prefer to talk about work, culture, and ordinary stuff first. This springs from a proper concern to not come off as stiff evangelists but as real, caring people. Many of us are slow to bring up the gospel with co-workers because we don't want people to feel like a spiritual project. Evangelicals have a terrible reputation for witnessing at work while neglecting their work. Work becomes a platform for evangelism, making people the real project. A helpful word for this is *proselytism*, a coercive attempt to get people to believe what we believe. Proselytizing aims at recruiting Non-Christians to our doctrine, our ethics, our political views or church but rarely to Jesus. People can smell proselytizing a mile away. It's a turn off. Imagine someone trying to coerce you to join their religion or political party. You wouldn't appreciate it.

Jesus teaches us to love not proselytize our neighbor. He invested heavily in relationships because he saw people in the image of God not as evangelistic projects. Treating people as spiritual projects misrepresents Jesus, not just in his approach to people, but also in his approach to vocation. As the agent of creation, Jesus deeply values what we do with his creation (our vocation). To reduce the workplace to a platform for evangelism is to reduce Jesus to a half-hearted redeemer, unconcerned with his creation. It separates what the Colossian hymn puts together — Jesus as creator and Jesus as redeemer, so that Jesus might be seen as preeminent in all things, not just evangelism (Col. 1:15-20). A lot of non-Christians find this kind of Christianity unattractive. They want to make great culture not abandon it. They also value relationships. Christians who dismiss the value of vocation and move on from relationships with non-Christians because they don't express interest in Jesus fail to represent Jesus. They reveal a truncated gospel. To this kind of Christian, recruitment - not relationship - is uppermost. They create the impression that Christianity is about impersonal, hyper-spiritual evangelism not caring relationships based on the love of Jesus. The world hears Jesus but sees religion. With this proselytizing Christianity hovering over the evangelical conscience, it is natural that many respond by emphasizing "relationships first."

# Love Not Proselytize Your Neighbor

The concern to have a relationship before sharing the gospel has some biblical warrant. Jesus said: "Love your neighbor," not proselytize your neighbor. To proselytize is to coerce or induce people to believe what you believe. The person who proselytizes *coerces* by forcefully defending and advancing their beliefs. Grabbing evidence and opportunities, Christians back their co-workers into a theological corner, expecting them to throw up their hands and say, "I believe!" Other times, proselytizing takes the form of *recruitment*. We might try to convince people to join our moral or political agenda, as if Jesus wants to add to his numbers to strengthen a political constituency.

When we proselytize people, we reduce discipleship to an intellectual enterprise. In effect, we replace the gospel with doctrinal agreement (or just being right). When we focus on recruitment, we make Christianity about power or morality. This replaces the gospel with religion or rightwing politics. But Paul shared a gospel that was all about Jesus, preaching Christ and him crucified (1 Cor. 2:1). He resolved to preach Christ not politics. Similarly, when sharing our faith, we need to make Jesus the stumbling block not morality or politics. When we put doctrinal, moral, and political blocks in front of the gospel, we proselytize instead of evangelize. I've had countless conversations with non-Christians where I had to remove these stumbling blocks before getting to the heart with the wonderful news of the gospel. Getting to the heart takes time. We need what Michael Frost calls "Slow Evangelism."[5] We need faith in God and love for people that slows us down to listen to others so that we can learn how to make the good news good to their bad news. For many, hearing that Jesus died on the cross for them is entirely irrelevant; we have to show the relevance of Jesus to their real need. Relationships are essential to discerning and meeting real needs. Remember the insight of Francis Schaeffer who advocated taking an hour with a non-Christian and listening for fifty-five minutes. Then, in the last five minutes, we will I have something to say. We often hesitate to share our faith because we want people to know that we value them, regardless of their response. But if we truly value them, we wont simply "wait" to share the gospel; we will also embody it by listening well.

## Wonderful Doesn't Wait

Should we always wait for a relationship to be formed? Have you noticed that when you encounter something truly wonderful, you don't always wait for a relationship to tell someone about it? There are things that are so urgent, so weighty, and so wonderful that we burst out to talk about them whether we have a

---

[5] Michael Frost, *The Road to Missional: Journey to the Center of the Church* (Grand Rapids, MI: Eerdmans, 2011), 41-62.

relationship or not! When our sports team scores to win the game, we don't look around the stadium and think: "I can tell people how happy I am about this win. I don't even know them!" No, we don't wait to express our joy; we burst out when our team wins. We celebrate with strangers and go nuts on social media. When we're at a concert and our favorite song is played, and the band is really rocking, we don't wait to sing along or comment. We sing and chat it up with strangers. After reading a book or seeing a great movie, perhaps *The Hunger Games*, we strike up conversation with people at work about how great the movie was. When we see great art, we call people over to view it with us. When something is truly wonderful, we often don't wait to talk about it. We become evangelists. Is the news about Jesus so urgent, weighty, and wonderful that we can't help but share it? It should be but often it isn't as exciting as the game, concert, book, movie, or work of art. Why? Very often this is because we aren't immersed in the goodness of the gospel. We aren't watching the gospel's every move, taking in its story, mesmerized by its characters, or soaking in its beauty. It is old, memorized, fading news because we haven't had a fresh encounter with Christ in weeks! The wonder is lost because we haven't plunged ourselves into the redemptive drama through worship, prayer, or Bible meditation. We are prone to talk about the gospel when the good news is good news to *us*.

## A Haircut and Union with Christ

I walked up to Birds Barbershop to get a haircut. It's kind of an Austin icon. Punk music, random furniture, wall art that requires 3-D glasses (which they provide), and, of course, service with an attitude. I'm in the heart of the counterculture. Before I sat down, they offered me the typical options: a Lone Star beer or a bottle of water. My usual hairdresser wasn't in, but my hair was overdue for a cut. I plopped down in the barber chair to get my haircut by a new hairdresser. Risky, I know. The things we do for the gospel!

After introducing myself, I asked Amber what she loved about cutting hair. We talked about her craft and the challenges that come along with it. Then came the fated question: "So what do you do?" "I'm a pastor of a church that gathers downtown, Austin City Life", I replied. Our vision is to bring life, not take life, from the city. Christians have a terrible reputation for being indifferent to the needs of the city. So we're devoting ourselves to renewing the city socially, spiritually, and culturally. This piqued her interest, so she asked for examples of what I was talking about. I shared various things we do in the city. I explained how our City Groups serve the marginalized through feeding the homeless, hanging out with fatherless kids, and mentoring children at a local shelter. I also mentioned our non-profit, Music for the City, which promotes the music of upcoming artists through compilation albums, festivals, and concerts. She thought it was cool.

I could have stopped there. Awesome. My hairdresser thinks church is cool; this is so rare. I could have proceeded to invite her to church, but union with Christ prompted me to do more. The gospel metaphor of union with Christ is the foundational doctrine through which all other saving doctrines flow. It refers to our mystical incorporation into the person of Christ such that we gain an entirely new identity. The many "in Christ" statements littered throughout Scripture designate this union. Ephesians chapter one shows us that all the heavenly blessings come rushing to us "in Christ Jesus" (1:3) including: election, grace, redemption, reconciliation, forgiveness, and sealing by the Spirit. This great work of God to include us in his plan of redemption is not a cold strategy but a warm soteriology. Union with Christ is, as it sounds—a deeply personal, affectionate relationship with Christ by Christ. It is about God in Christ living, suffering, dying, rising, and ascending in order to draw us up with him into the heavenly places where we enjoy perfect love, acceptance, and divine intimacy (Col. 3:1-4). When we are enjoying our union with Christ, it pokes out. We are prompted by the Spirit to be ourselves in Jesus.

As I sat in the chair, the Spirit prompted me to go beyond a church invitation. His love pressed against my vocal chords. At the risk of rejection, I spoke. I asked Amber if she had any religious background. She explained that her grandmother took her to church when she was young, but that she hadn't been in at least ten years. As she recalled, the people were nice but she just didn't see the relevance of church. It seemed so backwards, and out of touch with reality. People everywhere need to see the relevance of the gospel. This is especially true among progressive urbanites. Amber hadn't encountered a forward thinking, city-changing gospel until I sat in her chair. As hairs showered my lap, we continued to talk. Sensing the haircut was coming to a close, I circled back to our discussion about our church. I said: "You know, Amber, the reason I do all this stuff for the city isn't because I'm a great person. I'm not even a great pastor; it's because I have a great God. I've had a profound personal encounter with Jesus Christ and he's utterly changed me." Union with Christ prompted me to go public with the unparalleled joy of union with *Christ*. Sometimes, wonderful doesn't wait. We talk about what we are taken with.

If you recall, I had no relationship with Amber before sitting in her barber chair, and yet, in the span of forty-five minutes we had a meaningful conversation about life, vocation, church, and Christ. Did I put relationship first? Did I wait to share the gospel with her until she trusted me, knew my family, and had visited a church gathering? No, but love of God compelled me (2 Cor. 5:14). This was no exercise in coercion; it was the overflow of

45

union. I wasn't recruiting; I was rejoicing. If there's one thing urbanites can detect, it's in-authenticity. They are bombarded by uncaring ads, manipulative handbills, commercials, and spam all day long, so when authenticity happens, it stands out. From a place of affectionate union with Christ, I was able to love her in forty-five minutes in a way that would typically take longer. Why? Because I was soaking in the gospel. I spoke from a place of authentic love for Jesus. The love of Christ compelled me to ask her questions not announce my doctrines. I didn't lead off with a gospel presentation. Instead, I loved her like a person. I showed genuine interest in her craft, empathized with her objections regarding church, complimented her on my haircut, and tipped well.

My talk about Jesus was a direct result of questions she asked. I didn't hijack the conversation to shove my evangelical duty down her throat. Nor did I dodge the reasons for my concern about the city; I was honest about them. I also didn't prop myself up in self-righteousness; I didn't need to because Christ is my righteousness. What I sensed in the moment was genuine awe over what God is doing, so instead of giving credit to the church or myself, I gave credit to Jesus. Notice I didn't give credit in a canned way: "All the glory goes to God." What does "giving glory" mean to a hipster hairdresser anyway? I gave credit in a personal way. I could feel the Spirit stirring my affections for what Jesus has done for me and I wanted Amber to know him.

So I shared with her that it all boiled down to Jesus, a personal, profound encounter with Jesus. I talked about Jesus because I was taken with Jesus (which is *too* infrequent). I wasn't witnessing to Amber; Amber was witnessing Christ in me, the hope of glory (Col. 1:27)! My union with Christ was shining through.

We all talk about what we are taken with. You should know that not all my haircuts go like this! There are many days that I'm not taken with Jesus and, as a result, I wait to speak because I haven't seen Christ as wonderful. You see, we all need fresh encounters with Jesus for our evangelism to ring with authenticity. We need fresh encounters with Jesus to remain our authentic ourselves. Otherwise, we will begin to treat people as projects to be avoided or recruited. Evangelism will become a way to judge or praise ourselves. Apart from the gospel, evangelism will become a measuring stick not an overflow of joy in Christ. People can sense the stick but are struck by the joy. Amber was visibly impressed, not by me, but by the Savior. We don't always wait to talk about what is wonderful, but when we talk it will be full of love. In summary, the principle value behind "having a relationship first" can be preserved in evangelism when our talk of Christ arises from the love of Christ. Have you ever considered what would have happened if Jesus waited to offer the thief on the cross eternal life until he had a relationship with him? What if authors, pastors, and preachers waited to tell you the good news until they had a relationship with you? There are things so wonderful they don't deserve a wait!

# 4

# I Don't Want to Be Intolerant

Tolerance. Is it a virtue or a vice? Those who see tolerance as a virtue are slow to share their faith with others. They don't talk about the exclusive claims of Christ because they don't want to exclude others. Out of love, they don't want to demean other's beliefs. If you hold tolerance as a virtue, you believe that everyone deserves the right to believe what he or she believes. Alternatively, those who see tolerance as a vice are quick to engage or condemn other faiths. They insist on the exclusive claims of Christ and often dismiss the value of other religions. If you see tolerance as a vice, you are quick to insist there can only be one absolute truth. Who is right? How should we view tolerance?

## Tolerance as Christian Love

Tolerance can be either an expression of Christian love or an expression of relational (and intellectual) carelessness. How do you know if your tolerance is loving or careless? The answer depends on what we mean by tolerance. In *The Intolerance of Tolerance*, D. A. Carson helpfully clarifies the meaning of tolerance.[6] He points out that there are two types of tolerance: old and new. Old tolerance is the belief that other opinions *have a right to exist*. This is a very Christian notion. Jesus taught us to love our neighbor, and even our enemy. Jesus did not campaign against Greek philosophy and Roman Emperor worship. Jesus' ethic of love should compel disciples to tolerate other beliefs and religions. We ought to grant others the right to believe whatever they desire to believe. After all, what people believe is a deeply personal, profound matter. Settling on a religious belief isn't like picking out a ripe banana at the supermarket. Our beliefs require much more thought and investment. Love values people and their beliefs. It respects the things they hold dear. Since Christians are to love God, neighbor, and even our enemies, we should practice the old tolerance, winsomely granting people the right to hold beliefs different from our own. In this way, tolerance can be very loving and respectful. Following the

---

[6] D. A. Carson, *The Intolerance of Tolerance* (Grand Rapids, MI: Eerdmans, 2012).

pattern of Jesus, Christians should be loving and tolerant, not coercive or proselytizing.

## The Carelessness of Tolerance

The new tolerance is defined as the belief that *all opinions are equally valid or true.* This is quite a leap from the old tolerance. It is one thing to say something has the right to exist; it is quite another to say that two beliefs are equally valid. If we followed the logic of the new tolerance, it would be possible to affirm the following two statements:

- We should grant others the dignity to believe whatever they want to believe.
- We should force others to believe whatever we believe to be true.

The new tolerance has to allow for these two statements to coexist. This, of course, is impossible to do! The new tolerance is *intellectually* careless. The new tolerance carelessly dismisses careful logic. For instance, new tolerance affirms that both Jesus and Allah is God. It also affirms that working to keep the Five Pillars of Islam and trusting in the work of Christ are equally valid ways to get to God. The problem, however, is that both Islam and Christianity fundamentally disagree on who God is and how to reach him. In Islam, we reach up to God, but in

Christianity God reaches down to us. These beliefs can't be equally valid and true because they are contradictory. To affirm one is to invalidate the other.

This intellectual carelessness is not only illogical; it is exclusive and intolerant. The new tolerance exclusively claims that its policy of self-contradictory tolerance is the only way to view the world. This, of course, is intolerant. It refuses to practice the old tolerance, respecting differing views (exclusive and inclusive). Quite the opposite, new tolerance disrespects the differences between faiths. It denies the distinctive view and path to God laid out by age-old religions. Instead, the new tolerance makes the exclusive claim that all religions lead to the same God. This is an act of great disrespect, dismissing the centuries of study, formulation, adherence, and faith of various religious devotees. In this, the new tolerance is religious. It makes an exclusive claim (all beliefs are equally true) and intolerantly forces that belief onto everyone. As a result, this kind of tolerance is not only intellectually careless but also *relationally* careless.

## The Uniqueness of Christ on a Barstool

Living in Austin, I am frequently asked if I believe Jesus is the only way to God. Seventy-six percent of the people in the city center don't even believe Jesus is the Son of God, much less the only way to God. Making the exclusive claim that Jesus is the only way to God goes against the grain of the new tolerance. Yet, Jesus was unequivocal when it came to the way to the Father: "I am the way, and the truth, and the life. No one comes to the Father except through me" (Jn. 14:6). While Jesus granted people the dignity to believe whatever they wanted, he knew that it was faith in Him, alone, that could give them the dignity they needed. He insisted on his unique way to the Father all the way to the death.

It was one of our regular nights at the *Gingerman*, a low-lit, wood-paneled, leather chaired pub. I often met Dave here to talk about spiritual matters and enjoy his company. Tonight, he invited his friend Brian. When Brian turned up, we were in the thick of the gospel, a topic uncommon in Brian's conversation. He listened in. Then, Dave asked Brian, "So, man. What do you think about this?" After pontificating a bit, Brian asked me: "So what about the Muslims. I mean they're serious too. They are willing to die for what they believe. Are you saying that they won't go to heaven?" I responded by saying: "Brian, I respect these men for their sincerity. They are more serious about their faith than many Christians, but just because they are sincere doesn't mean they are right. Many people are sincerely wrong about all kinds of things. There were scientists who were sincerely wrong about the earth being the center of the universe. We shouldn't mistake sincerity for truth." I moved on to answer the question about the eternal destiny of sincere Muslims. As we talked, I encouraged him to evaluate the value of what Jesus said in John 14 based on truthfulness not sincerity. After sketching some of the major distinctions between Islam and Christianity, I made this simple observation about the uniqueness of Christ. "In all major world religions, a way is devised to work our way to the God. The problem, however, is that we can't keep all the rules and adhere to all the ways. We are imperfect. In Christianity, however, the God works his way down to us. He keeps all the rules; he makes the way. This is called grace. It is the fundamental difference between Christianity and other religions. So, sincere self-sacrifice, while noble, does not make one acceptable to a holy God. Rather, we need someone to sacrifice for our failures to honor the God and to present us acceptable to him. This is precisely what Jesus did. No other religion offers this, where the God gets hurt on behalf of his people, dies, rises from the dead and then makes them acceptable, forgiven, and righteous."

Christianity is utterly unique, not because Christians are better but because Christ is better. In Christianity, God dies so man can live. In other religions, generally speaking, men live in the uncertain hope that they won't really die. In the gospel, God works his way down to us in Jesus to bear our load and give us his life. In religion, man works his way up to God bearing an unbearable load with a vague hope of eternal life. Christ is utterly unique. He dies and lives again so that we can die and truly live. By faith, his death and resurrection become our death and resurrection. Jesus is the substitute sacrifice to substitute for us a better life. The self-sacrifice of God in Christ to reconcile estranged, indifferent, distrusting, and even hostile sinners is called *redemption*. Brian needed to hear how the gospel was unique in this respect. The gospel metaphor of redemption shows us not only the need for someone to pay the penalty for our sinful crimes, but also tells us that Christ paid it for us. When our sentence was passed, he stepped up to serve our sentence. He made atonement for our sins despite the fact that he, himself, had no sin. His sinless perfection and mind-blowing grace make him the utterly unique, exclusively gracious, and the one and only way to be reconciled to a holy God. To reject Jesus, as the only way to the Father is to reject our only way to be forgiven and redeemed: "In him, we have redemption through his blood, the forgiveness of our sins, according to the riches of his grace" (Eph. 1:7).

By explaining the gospel metaphor of redemption, I was able to communicate the uniqueness of Christ in comparison to other religions. I did not demean Islam or mock Muslim sincerity and religious fervor. In fact, I praised their sincerity. However, I also avoided intellectual carelessness. I avoided the fallacy of the new tolerance, where everything is equally true. In favor of the old tolerance, I honored what is honorable in Islam but moved onto the more important issue of the truth and uniqueness of the gospel of Jesus Christ. Brian did not repent on the spot; however, I did remove a stone by addressing one of his reasons for unbelief. Within a year he was engaged in a church, playing in worship bands regularly, and moving along in his faith.

So you see, there's quite a difference between the old and new tolerance. While we should grant others the dignity of their beliefs, classic tolerance also expects the differences between beliefs to come out. Classic (and Christian) tolerance should promote respectful dialogue and charitable debate between religions. Christians should honor other worldviews and dialogue with people of other faiths to grow in clarity and appreciation of distinctives. We should be eager to learn from others not be fearful or condemning of them. Meaningful conversation is in short supply, and of all people, Christians should have meaningful conversations with others. After all, Jesus claimed to answer the deepest questions of life. If his teachings are true, then we have every reason to talk deeply with others about meaning, faith, and truth. Jesus gives us every reason to be classically tolerant, full of love, and persuasively engaged in the things that matter most. When we winsomely and wisely show how the redemption of Christ is unique among world religions, we give people a gospel worth believing!

# 5

## I Don't Want to Be a Know-It-All

One of the most common concerns in evangelism is not having all the right answers. A lot of people are reluctant to talk about Christ because they are concerned they won't know how to respond to skeptical questions: "How can Jesus be the only way to God?" "Doesn't the Bible have lots of errors?" These are serious questions that deserve thoughtful responses. As Christians, we should have reasons for our hope. Alternatively, there are people who can answer many of these questions but come off as a know-it-all. Most people don't want to be a know-it-all. I wonder if our evangelistic fear (or arrogance) runs deeper than having the right answers. Is it possible we have *put our hope in possessing right answers* instead of *having right answers for an existing hope*? Let's consider the role of "right answers" in the difficulty of sharing our faith.

## Reasons for Hope

While some consider Christianity to be an unthinking faith, the Bible underscores the importance of reason. Peter, a disciple *not* known for being good with words, wrote this: "Have no fear of them, nor be troubled, but in your hearts honor Christ the Lord as holy, *always being prepared to make a defense to anyone who asks you for a reason for the hope that is in you*." (1 Pet. 3:14-15). We are to offer "reasons" for our hope, to always be prepared. Prepared to do what? "Make a defense" is a translation of the word from which we get *apologetic*. An apologetic isn't an "I'm sorry" attitude. Nor is it a defensive, antagonistic stance against culture. It is a reasoned statement of belief. To make an apologetic, then, isn't to argue out of defensive insecurity, but to offer a reasonable explanation from our security. What kind of security frees us to offer reasonable explanations for our faith?

Two kinds of security free us to engage in apologetics. The first is *intellectual security*. The Christian faith has a long tradition of apologists who have faithfully defended the faith century to century, often answering some of the same questions. Some of the earliest apologists include: Justin Martyr, Tertullian, Tatian, and Clement of Alexandria. Their apologetic answers have been handed down from generation to generation. New apologists such as Ravi Zacharias, William Lane Craig, Tim Keller, John

Frame, and Alvin Plantinga, also address new questions. We do well to read them.

However, the gospel alone, acts as a grand apologetic addressing the deepest of life's questions including: the value of creation, the problem of evil and suffering, the existence of God, the hope of salvation, the nature of God and man, and the role of faith. Through apologetics the gospel has been proven to be intellectually credible and existentially satisfying for many people across many cultures. The gospel provides a coherent, rational view on the world that provides intellectual security. It makes sense of a world where things are not as they are supposed to be. But there is another security that frees us to offer reasonable explanations for Christian faith.

## Deep Security

Many of us don't make time to read the old and new apologists. And perhaps we don't have to know them all? Is it possible that Peter had in mind an apologetics that included, not just reasons, but faith? Peter was writing to people who feared persecution for their faith. When we struggle to share our faith, do we not face persecution? When we engage in conversation with a skeptic (or just consider the prospect!), we often encounter feelings of inadequacy. We are attacked by thoughts that undermine our confidence, diminish our trust in Christ, and redirect us away from speaking about Jesus. "You won't have all the right answers." "Do you really think you can convince this person to trust Jesus?" "You should bring them a book instead or just let a smarter Christian talk to them." Surely this is spiritual persecution. Cultural apologist Ken Myers comments:

> The challenge of living with popular culture may well be as serious for modern Christians as persecution and plagues were for the saints of earlier centuries.[7]

These are challenging times. It can be difficult to answer objections and sympathize with skeptics when we feel so inadequate. It's tough to sort through all the pop philosophy and bumper sticker truth claims. This is why it is important that we look to teachers, pastors, authors, and disciplers to guide us through these challenges. We should have a reasonable defense for our faith. However, we have to make peace with the fact that we won't have the right answer for every question. Moreover, we need to consider if "having the right answer" is really the goal of biblical evangelism. Is possessing all the right answers really the expectation of Jesus? To be sure, we should have clarity on the gospel and how it is good news for others, but must everyone become a professional apologist? I don't think so. While we may not have the ability to answer every question, Jesus does give us the ability to always be secure in our faith. Disciples who are humbly secure in Jesus are compelling. That kind of faith is

---

[7] Ken Myers, *All God's Children and Blue Suede Shoes: Christians and Popular Culture* (Wheaton, IL: Crossway, 1989), v.

an apologetic in itself. When difficult questions are raised and doubts surface, we need a security deeper than our intellect and stronger than our persecution.

Before instructing the early Christians to always have an apologetic, Peter prefaces his statement with this: "Have no fear of them, nor be troubled, *but in your hearts honor Christ the Lord as holy...*" (1 Pet. 3:14). He reassures them, in the face of mockery, to sink their security deep into their hearts not their heads. True apologetics begins with heartfelt confidence in Jesus. When we fear what people might ask or say in response to our genuine statements about Jesus, right answers can't rescue us. You see, our security breech is deeper than the intellect; it runs right down into our hearts, where we do have fear of them, where we are inordinately troubled by what others think. Our reluctance to talk about Jesus often springs from honoring the approval of others in our hearts instead of resting our hearts in the approval of Christ the Lord. What we need is right answers for our misplaced hope.

## Adoption in a Kinko's

The gospel metaphor of adoption can do wonders for our fears. Adoption confers on us the undying approval of God the Father. It sweeps us into his family as his very own sons and daughters where, despite our failures, he loves us still. That's right. When you don't have the right answers, when you trust in the right answers and not in Him, and when you fail to obey him in any area of your life, his love endures. Adoption reminds us that salvation is warm, personal, and full of love. When we fail the Father, it is not as if he disapproving looks down from heaven shaking his finger. Because we are in Christ, he stands in front of us with arms wide open. He beckons us home. My goodness, like the father of the prodigal, he runs to us in reckless love (Luke 15:20)!

Paul tells us in Galatians that when we are adopted, our status changes from slave to son. Apart from Christ, we are enslaved to the "elementary principles of the world" (4:3). These principles hold power over us, often through the form of a worldly master or idea. We might be enslaved to the master of what others think about us. Or we may be enslaved to an idea-listic, relational fantasy where those around us meet our every emotional need. In both of these examples, we long for the approval of others instead of resting in the approval we have in Christ. This human approval is a kind of slavery. In evangelistic opportunities, it paralyzes us and keeps us from sharing the hope and love of Christ. One day I walked into a Kinko's to get a copy of a book manuscript. I had just returned from a Christian conference and was wearing the conference T-shirt. All of a sudden I was gripped with fearful thoughts. What if the Kinko's guy reads my T-shirt and asks me about "Gospel Communities on Mission?"

What will I say? Oh, and then there's my book. What if he reads the title, *Gospel-Centered Discipleship*? How will I explain it to a non-Christian in one minute? In that moment I was filled with fear about what this random Kinko's guy thought about me (not what he thought about Christ). I feared the loss of his approval— a complete stranger! How preposterous. You mean an author of two books about the gospel loses faith in the gospel? Oh yes, every single day, which is why I'm so deeply moved by God's enduring approval and love. I abandon it in a moment for the slavery of human approval, but still he loves me.

Some people don't struggle with approval in evangelism. In fact, they are quite confident they have the answers. They are so confident that their arrogance comes through when they talk about spiritual things. They try to beat people out in arguments no matter what the cost. They lose their cool in the process. They may even resort to attacking statements. This stacks obstacles in front of the gospel. What is awry here? This confidence rests in the wrong place. It is a sure sign that hope is misplaced. Their hope is in possessing the right answers not in being possessed by a righteous God. How do I know? One reason is that I have been that guy. Insensitive and uncaring, I have stomped on hearts in my quest to impress minds. This was motivated, not by a desire for approval, but for applause. Another reason is because faith in the gospel produces humble confidence. It humbles us because we know we are undeserving, just like the people around us. It lifts us up because, in Christ, we get infinitely more than we deserve. The gospel is incredibly humbling if you think about it. I was so sinful God had to die for me, but God is so gracious he both dies and lives for me. We hit the gospel jackpot by the grace of God. As a result, we are humbled that God would sweep us into his family but confident Christ is enough to get us there. Hope in Jesus keeps us from arrogance because we don't hang our worth on right answers. Instead, our worth rests in what Jesus has done for us.

Adoption is a change in status from slave to son or daughter. How does this happen? Through the Spirit of God: *"God has sent the Spirit of his Son into our hearts, crying, "Abba! Father! So you are no longer a slave, but a son, and if a son, then an heir through God."* (3:6-7). The Spirit doesn't just give us a new status; he gives us a voice before our Creator. The Spirit of the Son who cries out "Abba! Father!" The word "Abba" is probably an Aramaic word for "dearest Father", which is uniquely used by Jesus in Scripture (Matt 6:9; John 14:21; 20:17). We have a voice before Father God because of the Spirit and the Son. He listens to our fears, receives our repentance, and gives us never-ending worth. When we are adopted into the Father's family, we move beyond relating to God as Judge into relating to him as dearest Father. We need not fear the judgment of others. The Father wants us to enjoy his approval more than the approval of others. He wants us to see how his love is superior to the love of others:

*"See what kind of love the Father has given to us, that we should be called children of God; and so we are"* (1 Jn. 3:1). The Spirit gives us a voice before the Father, the voice of a son not a slave.

This is why it is so important we keep in step with the Spirit (5:25). The Spirit walks slowly, gently moving us from intellectual security to heart security, as the truth of adoption slowly sinks in. The spirit of our age moves quickly. We need to slow down with the Spirit, allowing him to grasp our hand and guide us into gospel meditation and prayer, where we our adoption becomes a heart-convincing reality. If we slow down, we can hear his voice continually reminding us that we are sons not slaves, loved not judged. False masters and fleeting ideas quickly bombard us with lies, which is why praying throughout the day "in the Spirit" (Eph. 6:18) is such a powerful weapon for fighting off the fear of men. When the fear of man whispers discouragement, but the Spirit brings encouragement. When Satan whispers disapproval, the Spirit champions undying approval. Paul saw this connection between praying in the Spirit and proclaiming the gospel. He was so convinced of prayer in the Spirit, and aware of his weakness in the flesh, he asked the Ephesian church to pray: "that words may be given to me in opening my mouth boldly to proclaim the mystery of the gospel" (6:19).

The more we "honor Christ the Lord in our hearts", resting in his perfect approval, the less our hearts will treasure the approval or applause of others. The more we run our hearts under the waterfall of the heart-thrilling truth of adoption, the more we will overflow in humble confidence, not fear or arrogance. We will be less concerned about right answers and more concerned about Christ. Jesus is the better, more merciful Master and the gospel, the infinitely better idea. Jesus provides an impenetrable security and the gospel, an unwavering confidence. Peter reminds the suffering Christians that they have nothing to fear because they have Christ who offers perfect peace. He makes apologetics about Jesus, not merely right answers. The humble confidence of a gospel-centered disciple is an apologetic in its own right. These kinds of Christians generate a compelling, winsome witness. People may reject us but our forever acceptance in Christ gives us every reason to speak of him, of his grace, mercy, kindness, love, and triumph over sin, death, and evil. O for stronger men and women who sink their identity deeply into what Jesus says about us more than what peers and co-workers (might) say about us! Our silence will convince no one of rich, rewarding faith in Jesus. Fear over co-worker frowns will not inspire a smiling faith.

# Authentic Apologetics

Making a defense for the gospel is first about staying true to identity as child of God. Will we speak of our unique community in the church, the God-intoxicating gathering on Sunday, the stirring time of meditation on Wednesday morning, and the quiet, soul stirrings of communion with God? Will we speak authentically about what matters most to us and of the meaningful events in our lives or will we prove inauthentic, dismissing these things from conversation, and along with them, dismissing our true selves? Will we refrain from honoring the Lord Christ as holy in our hearts because we hold in honor the passing frowns of men in our heads? Surely the gospel offers a deeper security than the approval of passing men and women? Does not Christ's love run deeper, his acceptance purer, and his approval longer than the love, acceptance, and approval that any person could ever give? If so, apologetics is meant to spring from a deep security in the heart where, as adopted sons and daughters, the Spirit champions us as fully loved, fully accepted. Apologetics is a matter of the heart as well as the head.

Defending the faith, then, is as much about defending Christ as our Lord in our hearts as it is explaining the reasonableness of our faith. The goal of apologetics should never be to convert others (that is the Spirit's job), but it is to honor Christ as Lord in our hearts. This happens, very often, with our mouths. And in the end, the bottom-line issue isn't an intellectual objection but hope objection. We refuse to remove our hope from one thing and transfer it to the ultimate thing, the person of Jesus. Witnessing a person who hopes in Christ will be more compelling than any intellectual argument we could ever articulate. People need to see our hope burn in our bones. They need to sense the Lord Christ set apart in our hearts. They need to see that the gospel not only makes sense but that it also works. Christian faith is intellectually satisfying and existentially rich. So let's not put our hope in having right answers but have answers that reflect our hope.

# 6

## Sharing a Believable Gospel

So far we have examined four evangelistic concerns: coming off as preachy, being impersonal, failing to be tolerant, and not having the right answers. I will conclude with the fifth below. There is warrant for each concern. When the gospel is communicated in preachy, impersonal, intolerant, know-it-all ways, people find it hard to believe. Moreover, the gospel communicated with these attitudes is hardly worth believing. Typically, this style of evangelism is reduced to information. We content ourselves with "name-dropping" Jesus or telling people what Jesus has done for them. Evangelism devolves into a spiritual project for which we receive a √, √-, or √+. This is woefully inadequate. Worse, it is utterly unbelievable.

Telling people to "believe in Jesus" simply recites a memorized phrase not ministers the gospel. People want to know *why* the gospel is worth believing. The first place they look is your life. Are you gripped by the message of grace or by the anxieties of family? Does your character reflect the sacrifice and beauty of

Christ or the values of a capitalist society? Do you tower over others in pride; cower from them in fear, or do you possess a humble confidence that arises from your deep security in Christ? The second place people look is into or through our words. In the information age, people are used to seeing through words. Most evangelism offers a sound bite gospel, which is easily screened, distrusted, and dismissed. In order for people to see something of substance in our words, our gospel communication needs depth.

## New Creation in Rehab

Returning to Ben's story from chapter one, I was immediately confronted with the need for depth. Ben had been through hell and back as an addict and he was worn out, at the end of his rope, and ready for a new start. Name-dropping Jesus wouldn't cut it. First, he needed to see and feel the gospel. I desperately wanted to embody the love of Christ and I prayed he would feel and see it. Instead of correcting his life choices, I needed to understand his life choices. Sitting at rehab with him, I asked him questions: "What was your childhood like? When the church rejected you, did you experience rejection from your parents also? How did that make you feel? What was your drug community like? What were you looking for in this journey?" I asked these questions because I cared about Ben. This wasn't an evangelistic formula; it was a budding relationship with a man made in the image of God who was struggling to make sense of his life. I expressed empathy, concern, and compassion. He shared that he was adopted by good parents but struggled with a sense of loneliness and rejection. He began using drugs at age nine. Eventually we got down to the heart of the matter. "Ben, what have you been searching for?" He talked about loneliness and disappointment. I asked him how he thought God could figure into his longings. He wasn't sure. There was a strong sense that he was tired of the old life. He wanted to escape the broken, cemetery life. He wanted a new start. He wanted to know that a brighter future was possible. Ben needed to hear the gospel of new creation. Discerning some of his longings, I knew the promise of new creation could make the gospel a little more believable. He needed to know that there was a grace that could run deeper than all his failures and remake him from the inside out.

Understandably, a cloud of skepticism still hung over him. At the risk of rejection, I told him something like: "Ben, I know you're tired and worn out. I know this isn't what you hoped for your life and I want you know that God loves you. He wants to make you new. He wants to exile the old life and give you a new life in Jesus. Jesus died to give you this life, to forgive you and shower you with his grace. He wants you to come back home to enjoy his love, acceptance and peace. Instead of trusting in the escape of drugs and the fleeting acceptance of a drug community, he wants you to trust in Christ to be come a new creation, to be

71

remade from the inside out." He needed to know that his old man could be exiled and a new man could emerge (1 Cor. 5:17-18; cf. Col. 3:9-10; Eph. 4:20-24; Gal. 6:15). If nothing else, I knew the hope of new creation would be desirable and, most of all, I knew it was true. We talked about his struggle to believe it, to believe in God and to trust the person of Christ. I asked if he would be willing to talk to God about it. He said yes. We got him a Bible and prayed.

A shallow gospel wouldn't cut it with Ben, not with what he'd been through. His addiction ran deep and he needed a deep gospel. Hearing the information of Jesus' death on the cross would be screened and dismissed. He needed to know how Jesus' life and death is good news *in his life*. He needed a believable gospel. Two years later, Ben stood up in one of our Sunday church gatherings. Healthy, calm, and composed, he kicked the doors off of his private struggles and shared the story of his addiction and recovery. You could hear a pin drop. He talked about his struggle to find meaning and acceptance. When we asked him, "What's changed in what you believe about Jesus?" He responded: "Well, now *I do believe*. I have received his grace. I know that I'm forgiven for all I've done and that God wants to *know* me." Hallelujah! Ben has a growing addiction to grace. The Father knows him more deeply and perfectly than anyone else could know and love him. When asked, "How has God's grace been generous to you?" Ben responded: "Just being able to start *new*." New creation! For Ben, God's grace equals being new, liberated from the old life to experience an entirely new life in Christ. He went on: "It seems like such a long time ago…I feel like that person is way in the past…it amazes me that I could have grown so much in a year and a half." The old man exiled; the new man arrived! Belief in the gospel of new creation has made Ben new. The hope of new creation resonated with his longings; it pulled him towards Jesus. As he turned toward Christ, he experienced sorrow for his sins and joy for his forgiveness. He has moved away from rejection and into deep acceptance and love in Christ. He found a deep, not shallow, gospel. Ben now spends his time baking for others, keeping the prayer list for his City Group, going to recovery and counseling, and just being his new self.

## One Gospel Metaphor is Not Enough

Like all of us, Ben continues to work out his new life in Christ. He is tempted to return to exile. Fortunately, God does not demand perfection overnight but calls us preserving faith over a lifetime. Getting to Christ and persevering in Christ requires more than one gospel metaphor. One gospel metaphor is not enough. We need all of the gospel metaphors to bring us into union with Christ. We need all the benefits of Jesus' life, death, resurrection, and reign. In this short account of Ben's story, we see elements of redemption, justification, adoption, and new creation.

By focusing on one gospel metaphor in each story, I am not saying that one gospel metaphor is sufficient for salvation. Rather, I am suggesting there are some gospel metaphors that will prove more compelling than others. There are struggles and hopes, fears and dreams that sit on the surface of our stories. In gospel conversations, we get to do the loving, patient, and discerning work of listening well to people's stories. If we do listen with dependence on the Holy Spirit, the gospel metaphors that people need to hear can surface. We can discern how the good news is good in their bad news or how the good news is better than their best news. We can communicate a believable gospel.

Using the gospel for *how* we share the gospel, we have discerned five ways to communicate a believable gospel:

- To those searching for acceptance in all the wrong places, we can point them to perfect acceptance in the gospel of *justification*.
- To those searching for fulfilling relationships, we can point them to profound, personal *union with Christ*.
- To those who struggle with tolerance, we can show them the uniqueness of Christ in the gospel of *redemption*.

- To those who fear disapproval or demand the applause of others, we can share the gospel of *adoption*, which offers an enduring approval and produces humble confidence.
- To anyone longing for a new start, there is the hope of *new creation*.

Gospel theology should affect our evangelistic methodology. People don't what to hear a memorized presentation. They want to know how the gospel is good new *to them*. But first, the gospel needs to be good news to us. It is terribly difficult to be convincing about a belief when it is shared dispassionately. As we have seen, the gospel is good news for both the Christian and the non-Christian. We are all in need of grace. In fact, grace needs to make its way into our evangelism. Too often we put barriers in front of the gospel by the way we communicate the gospel. Hence the evangelistic concerns. Each gospel metaphor brings a grace-soaked correction to the five evangelistic concerns:

- Instead of preachy self-righteousness, we can point people to Christ's righteousness, which is based on his performance not ours.
- Instead of impersonal evangelism, we can share the hope of Jesus from our personal union with Christ.

- Instead of being intolerant, we can lovingly tolerate differences between religions while also communicating the unique, redeeming work of Christ.
- Instead of using right answers to gain approval or applause, we can share an enduring approval that comes through faith in the Father who adopts through the Son.
- Instead of sharing a shallow gospel of information, we can communicate the deep, transformative gospel of new creation.

In conclusion, we have seen the gospel is not only the evangelistic message but also provides an evangelistic method—gospel metaphors. These timeless metaphors communicate various aspects of God's saving grace to people in real space and time. Gospel communication comes in all kinds of forms—conversation, debate, teaching, and preaching. God has called us to join him by communicating the gospel to all peoples and then the end will come (Mk 24:14).

> And how are they to believe in him of whom they have never heard? And how are they to hear without someone preaching? And how are they to preach unless they are sent? (Rom. 10:14-15)

God has sent us on his grand mission. You are the most effective missionary to the people you live, work, and play with. You need not fear the disapproval of man because you have the enduring approval of God in Christ. You do not need the power of coercion or right answers because the power for salvation does not rest in methods but in the gospel itself: "For I am not ashamed of the gospel, for it is the power of God for salvation to everyone who believes" (Rom. 1:16). The gospel metaphors of justification, redemption, adoption, and new creation culminate in otherworldly power to bring sinners into heart-thrilling union with Christ. May we set the Lord Christ apart in our hearts, ready to give an authentic answer for the hope that is in us. *To God be the glory.*

## Jonathan K. Dodson

Jonathan Dodson (M.Div, ThM) is the founding pastor of City Life church in Austin, Tx which he started with his wife, Robie, and three children. As a recipient of God's grace, he enjoys communicating the gospel of Jesus and seeing Christ formed in others. He is also author of *Gospel-Centered Discipleship* available from Crossway Books.

- WE ARE -

We exist to see the world saturated with the Gospel so that every man, woman, and child has a daily encounter with Jesus through word or deed.

We desire to establish a family of churches committed to making disciples who make disciples to the glory of God.

*Learn more at:*

**WEARESOMA.COM**